An Excellent Facsimile of Beautiful Acient Ou-Yang Xun's Calligraphy

古欧阳询書法傑出典範摹本

Edited by
Raymond F. Gao and Johnson K. Gao

Front cover:
It used an aclyric painting by Johnson Gao, called as "Pu Tuo Island in the East Sea". That painting was based on his original water-color painting painted in 1961. There are two persons on the sand beach picking shells. That means two editors had picked beautiful shells from the "sea of calligraphy" to show you with this book. Due to the global warming and raised up sea level, those two big stones in the art are now disappeared or sank in to the sea in a recet visiting by Johnson K. Gao to the same place ot that Island in 2009.

Published by e-Pollination Inc. in 2015, USA.
Printed by lulu.com.

An Excellent Facsimile of Beautiful Acient Ou-Yang Xun's Calligraphy

Edited by
Raymond F. Gao & Johnson K. Gao

2015. USA

古欧阳询書法傑出典範摹本

高雷梦 高強生 編輯

2015 年於美國

獻給世界各地中國書法愛好者.

To Chinese calligraphy lovers the world over.

Preface

This book was jointly edited by Raymond F. Gao (son) and Johnson K. Gao (father) from a collection of antique calligraphic sheets of real handwriting. The first sheet of the original art was missing. Due to the long time storage and miss-arrangement, some of page numbers may be incorrect in sequence. Each original sheet looks like a - square-shaped frame of 28 x 28 cm, with 8 x 8 character spaces. There is a vertical folding line in the middle of it, which is now devided it into two pages. The left page, which has a thick frame in its top/left/bottom, appears first in the even nunber of page; followed by the right page, which has a thick frame in its top/right/bottom, appears in the following odd nunber of page.

The original model was written by Ouyang Xun. His Chinese name was 欧阳询。Mr. Ouyang Xun was born in 557 A. D. (the Liang Jin Di of South Dynasty, the Taiping 2nd year). He was the grandson of Ouyang Hui, the Da Si Kong of Chen Dynasty. Ouyang Xun's appearance is very ugly, but his calligraphy was known all over nations. People were eagerly interested in his handwritten words and letters, and considered them to be a treasure when they got them, and used them as their own writing model. Emperor Tang Gaozu expressed with a sigh: "I didn't expected that Ouyang Xun's reputation was so distantly dispersed. Even minority people like Yi and Di all knew him. After reviewing Ouyang Xun's handwriting, people might assume that he was an heroic big man in appearance and body." Wu De 7th year, Ouyang Xun obeyed the Emperor's order to edit 100 volumes of "The Collection of Art and Literature" together with Pei Yu and Chen Su-da. After finishing that book, he was rewarded with 200 bolts of cloth. Emperor Taizong Zhenguan early years, Ouyang Xun was up-ranked as the official title of Prince's Shui-geng-ling (and thus he was also known as Ouyang Shui-geng), he was offered a post of Hong Wen Musium's scholar, the Bohai county baron. He was died in 85 years of age.

The model was facsimiled (re-written) by Xie Jie-ru (謝介如), who might be born and lived in Suzhou (蘇州), because the post remark wrote that he was a man of Changzhou (長洲) , which is now called as Suzhou. The post remark was written by Yi Shi, in the Xuantong Dynesty (宣統 A.D. 1909-1911). Yi Shi's Chinese name is 綺石 (殺綺, or, 殺綺石室主). His formal name is Wang Bang-shou (王邦綬), born in Kunshan (昆山), who had worked in the Empiror's Academy (翰林院) in the late Qing Dynasty. 翰林院 was an academic and administrative institution. Membership in the academy was confined to an elite group of scholars, who performed secretarial and literary tasks for the court. To Wang Bang-shou, Raymond F. Gao shall call him grand-grand father.

序言

这本书是从真正的手写古色古香的书法版面掃描汇集而成，由高雷梦(儿子)和高强生(父亲)共同编辑。原始艺术的第一页失踪。由于很长时间存放和错差安排，一些页数也许顺序不一定正确。每一原始版面看起来象一个正方形框架，28x28 厘米，8x8 字符空间。在它中间有一条垂直的折叠的中线，现在将每一原始的版面划分成两页。左页，在它顶面/左边/底部有一个厚实的框架，首先勘印于双数页面，跟随的是右页，在它顶面/右边/底部有一个厚实的框架，勘印于跟随的单数页面。

原文由欧阳询所写。欧阳询生于 557 年 (南朝梁敬帝太平二年)，是陈朝大司空欧阳頠的孙子。欧阳询的形貌很丑陋，但他的书法却誉满天下，人们都争着想得到他亲笔书写的尺牍文字，一旦得到就视作瑰宝，作为自己习字的范本。唐高祖李渊感叹地说:"没想到欧阳询的名声竟大到连远方的夷狄都知道。他们看到欧阳询的笔迹，一定以为他是位形貌魁梧的人物吧。"武德七年，欧阳询奉诏与裴矩、陈叔达修撰《艺文类聚》100 卷。书成后，得到赏赐帛二百段。唐太宗贞观初年，欧阳询升为太子率更令（因而他又被称为欧阳率更），弘文馆学士，封渤海县男爵。八十五岁时辞世。

帖的主要部分由謝介如复抄，也许謝出生和住在苏州，因为书跋评论说他是長洲人，现在長洲叫作为苏州。书跋由綺石写在宣统年间(A.D.1909~1911)。綺石的中文名字是殺綺或者殺綺石室主。他的正式名字是王邦綏，昆山人，清宫末期他在翰林院做事。翰林院是一个学术和行政机关。翰林院的会员资格被限制在精英学者，执行朝廷的秘书和文艺任务。对王邦綏来说，高雷梦将称他为曾祖父。

Contents

(Note: The traditional way of reading Chinese characters in an assay is from the right side to the left side and from the top to the bottom. So, for pages 12-61, readers have to read characters of the odd pages first in the right side then to read the reversed even pages in the left side.)

1. Xie Jie-ru's hand script of the Ouyang Xun's original calligraphy

常豈若豐起蕭墻禍

生蕃翰強踰七國勢

重三監其有蹈水火

而不辟臨鋒刃而莫

於疾風艸世艱雲忠
臣彰於赴難衛須授
命結纓殉國英聲煥
于記牒徽烈著於旍

也昔立劾長邱樹績

東郡太尉裂壤於槐

里司徒胙土於門

是以車服旌其器骸

顧激清風於後葉抗
名節於當時者見之
弘義明公矣君諱誕
字玄憲安定朝那人

言曽祖重華使持
節龍驤將軍梁州刺
史潤木暉山方重價
於趙璧媚川照闕曜

茅社表其勳德銘功

衛鼎騰美晉鍾盛族

冠於國高華宗邁於

察邵備在史牒可略

17

剌史高衢將騁邊灰

追風之足扶搖始搏

早隆垂天之羽父璠

使持節驃騎大將軍

奇采於隨珠和雜

州贊治贈使持節散

騎常侍車騎大將軍

儀同三司縢涇二州

包申伯粟嵩山之秀
氣材無蕭相降昂緯
之淵精擾德依仁居
貞體道合章表質誣

開府儀同三司隨州
刺史長樂恭侯橫劍
桱枏威重冠軍折瑞
蕃條聲高勃海公量

於滇海博韜骨産文
贍卿雲孝窮溫清之
方忠盡匡救之道同
何充之器局被重晉

待爨於、朱藍恭孝為
基寧取訓於橋梓鋒
剌犀象百練挺於昆
吾翼掩鴛鴻九萬奮

榮名蕃牧則位重首·
寮祗服睢陽則譽光
上客既而蒼精委馭
炎運啓畺作貳邊脈

君類苟攸之宏畐見
知魏主斯故包羅衆
藝囊括群英者也起
家除周畢王府長史

霧維城寄深磐石建
旂玉壘作鎮銅梁妙
擇奇材以為僚佐授
公益州揔管府司法

寔資令望授廣州長
史悦近来遠竇輕訬
於雕題伐叛懷柔漸
淳化於緩耳蜀王地

古方今彼此一也尋
除尚書比部侍郎轉
刑部侍郎趨少紫庭
光暎朝列折旋丹地

昔梁孝開國首辟鄴

陽燕昭建邦肇徵郭

陜故得馳令問於碣

館播芳獻於平臺以

待旦志在恤刑呪綱
泣辜情存緩獄授大
理少卿公巨細必察
同張季之聽理寬猛

譽重周行俄遷治書
侍御史彈違紏愿時
絕權豪霜簡直繩俗
竅貪競隨文帝求衣

政術深曉治方減否
自分條目咸理丁母
憂去職哀慟里閭隣
人為之罷社悲感衢

相濟比于公之無究
但禮闈務殷樞轄寄
重允膺此職寔難其
人授尚書右丞洞明

詔奪情復其舊任于
時山東之地俗異民
澆雖預編民未行聲
教詔公持節為河北

34

路行客以之輟歌孝
德則師範彝倫精誠
則貫徹幽顯雖高曾
之至性何以加焉尋

榮甚繡衣之使事記
反命授尚書左丞然
并州地震衆墟城臨
晉水作固同於西蜀

河南道安撫大使仍
賜米五百石絹五百
匹公輶軒布政美冠
皇華之篇擁節觀風

公贇務大邦聲名藉

甚精民感化黠吏畏

咸屬文帝劔璽空留

鏖蹕莫反楊諒率太

設險類於東泰寔山
河之要衝信蕃服之
襟帶授公并州揔管
府司馬加儀同三司

奪宗之心公備說安

危具陳達順翻納魏

勃之榮反被王悍之

災仁壽四年九月盡

原之甲攤河玥之兵
方州叚之作亂京城
同州吁之挺禍濮上
雖無當辟之地乃懷

之棟折贈柱國左光
祿大夫封弘義郡公
食邑五千戶謚曰明
公禮也喪事所須隨

孔氏之山頹痛楊君
百辟興喪予之悲切
一萬機起殲良之歎
從運往春秋五十有

之采行己窮於六本
蘊德包於四科延閣
曲臺之奇書鴻都石
渠之秘說莫不尋其

由資給賜帛五千段粟三千石惟公溫潤成性鳳表白虹之珎蕭劂為文务挺雕龍

識待其舉火進賢方

於推轂知己俟以彈

冠存信捨原黃金賊

於然諾忘身殉難性

枝葉踐其隩隅辟越

箭達犀飾之以括羽

楚金切玉加之以磨

礱救之同於指囷親

采泰階黎綜機務豈
謂世逢多故運屬道
消未展經邦之謀奋
鍾非命之酷世子民

命輕於鴻毛齊大小
於沖襟混寵辱於靈
府可謂楷模雅俗冠
冕時雄者也方當亮

墓乃雕戈勒石騰實
飛聲樹之康衢永表
芳烈庶葛亮之隴鍾
生禁之以樵蘇賈逵

部尚書上柱國滑國
公無逸以為邢山之
下莫識祭仲之墳千
陵之東誰知子孟之

逢時翼主膺期佐帝
運榮經繪執鈞匡濟
門承積慶世挺偉人
夜光愧寶朝采慭珠

之碑魏君歎之以不
朽乃為銘曰
殷后華宗名卿冑系
人物代德衣冠重世

名馳碣石聲高建禮

珥筆憲臺握蘭文陛

分星裂土建侯開國

輔藉正人相資懿德

雲中比陸日下方苟
抑揚元輔黎賛機鈞
王葉東封貳圖北啓
伏奏青蒲申裾朱邱

建德劼節叀吾盡忠
命屯道著身殁名隆
牛亭始卜馬獨初封
翠碑刻鳳丹旂圖龍

中臺輟務晉陽就職

望重府朝譽聞宸極

亂階夢草災生剪桐

成師攝難太朴興戎

煙橫古樹雲鎖高松

敬銘盛德永播笙鏞

銀青光祿大夫

歐陽詢書

2. Wang Bang-shou's post remark

蘇黄米蔡此學唐之不如學宋而以

宋時石刻近今書有完好拓本如今

介如先生彈數十年精力心摹手追不

啻趨歐陽兩生之學者得有如此摹

本則又奚必學宋而不學唐哉

宣統建元己酉穀僑石室主跋

此長洲謙介如先生摹本唐時石刻
近今絕無善本予謂今之學書者
徒於唐碑中求盖雖美自宋以下善
本尚多盖因年代太久雖以翻刻止
谷字跡漫漶殘損不完故予勸後之
學書者與其學歐褚顏柳不若學

63

3. Four Attachments
selected by authors:

(3.1). Wei Zhi-jie's Calligraphy
(3.2). Catherine Gao's Calligraphy
(3.3). Johnson Gao's Calligraphy
(3.4). Raymond Gao's Poem of
"Monaco"

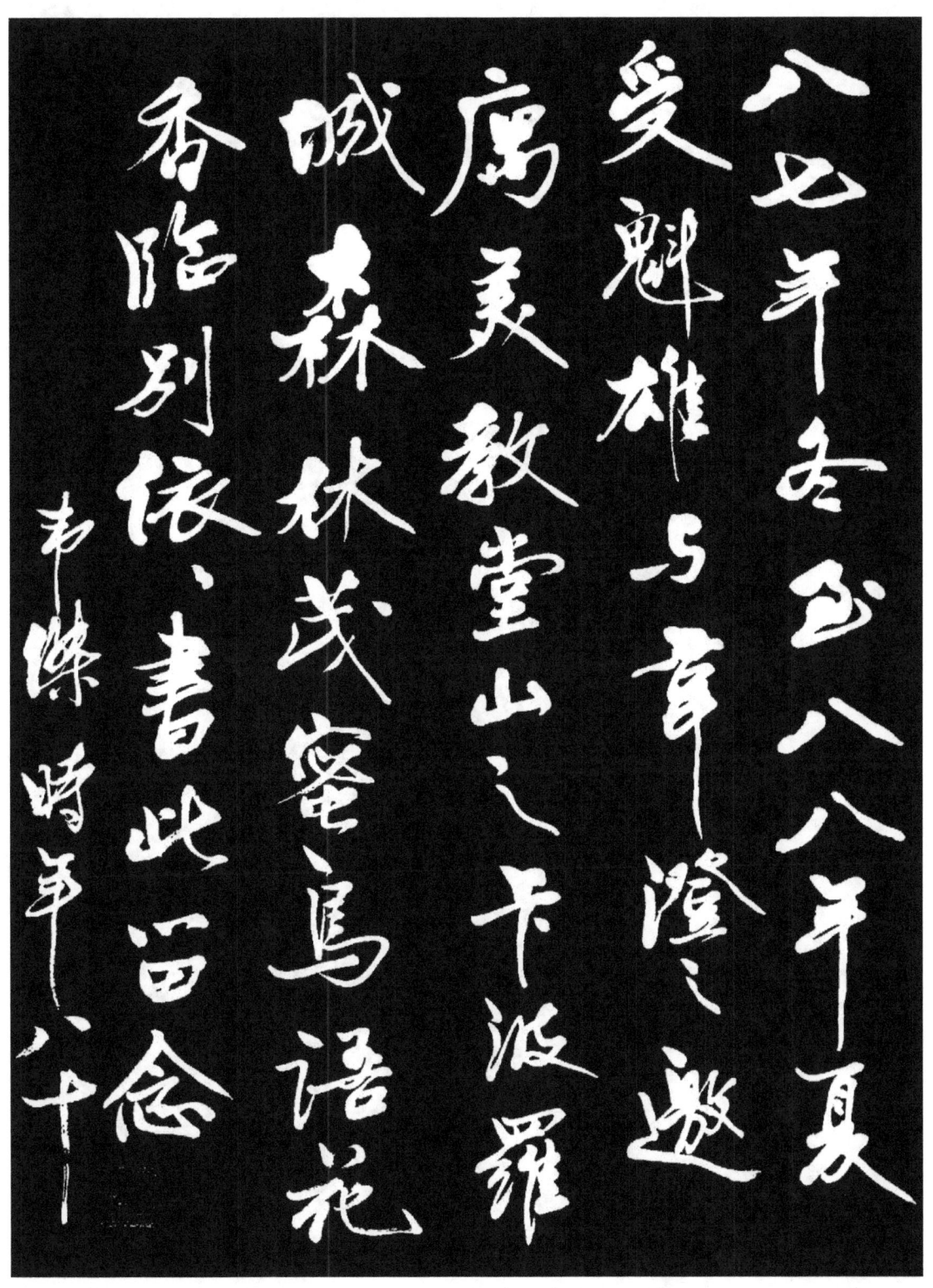

3.1. Calligraphy by Wei Zhi-jie (Wang Bang-shou's son-in-law), written in Chapel Hill, North Carolina, USA, 1987 at age of eighty.

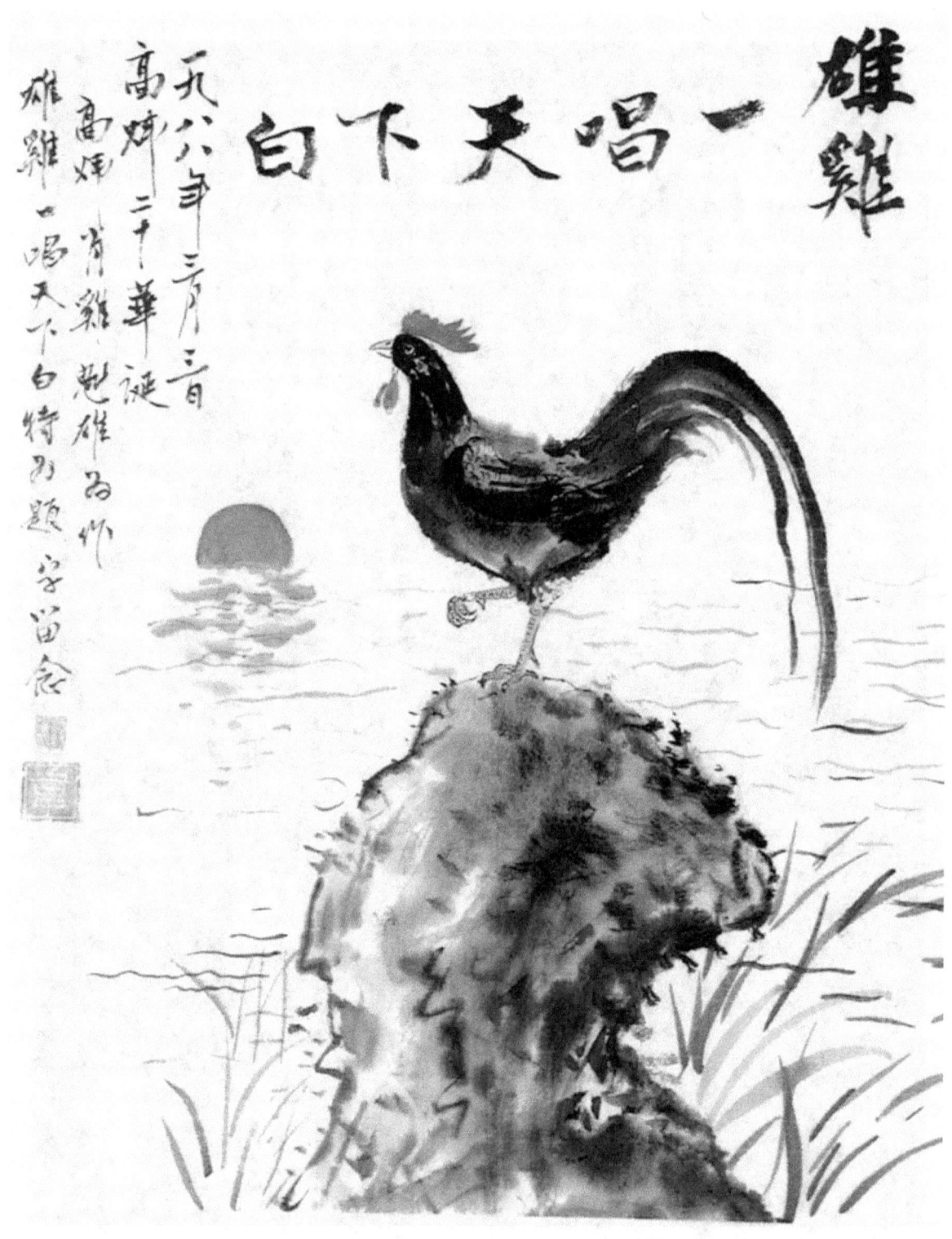

一 唱 天 下 白　　雄雞

天八年三月三日
高焯二十華誕
高焯 肖雞 魁雄為川
雄雞一喝天下白特乃題字 曲念

Calligraphy by Wei Zhi-jie (Wang Bang-shou's son-in-law), written in Chapel Hill, North Carolina, USA, 1988, at age of eighty, for his grandson Alvin W. Gao's 20 years birthday. That Chinese painting (11.75 x 14.5 inch) was painted by Johnson K. Gao.

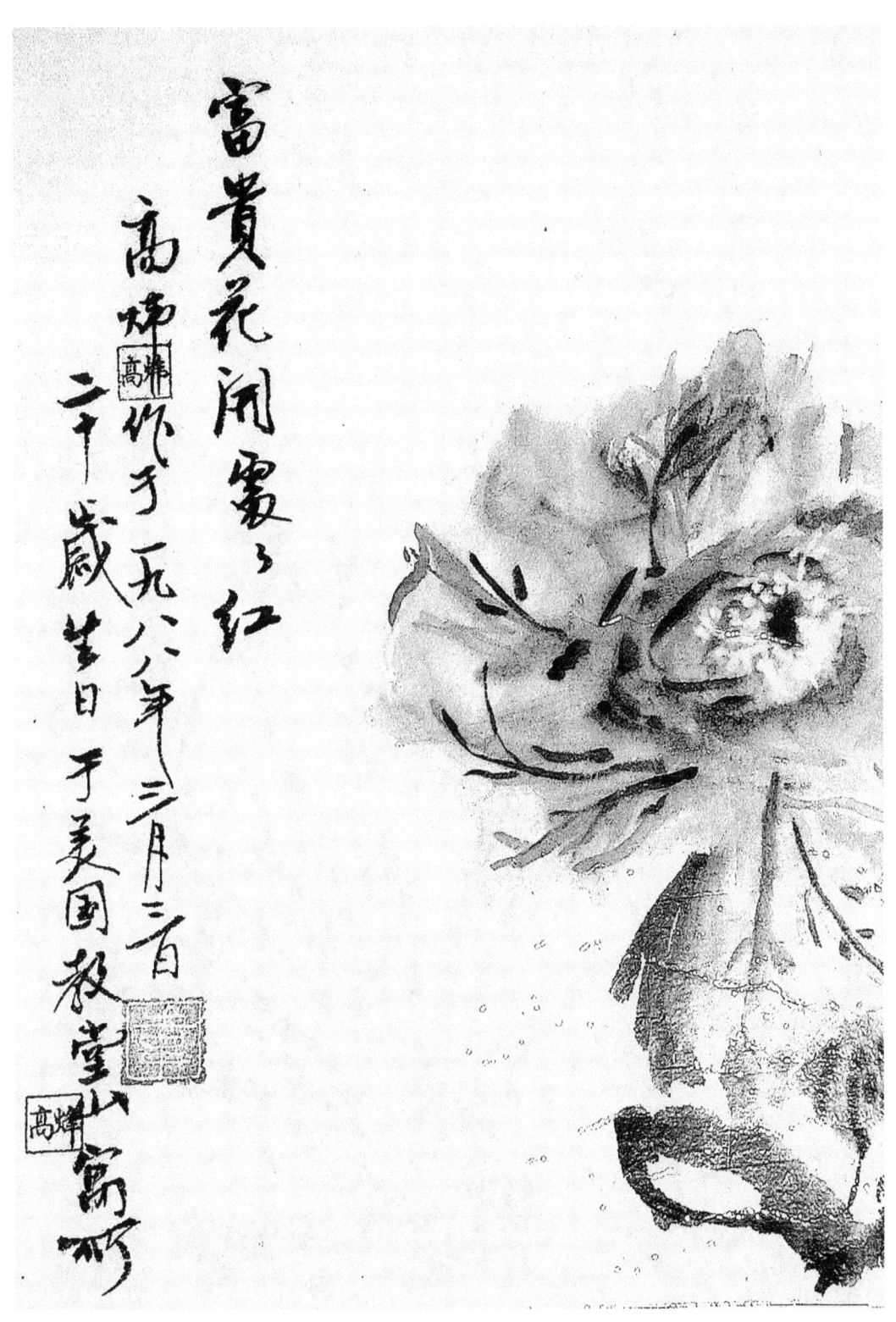

富貴花開霞霞紅

高煒作于一九八八年三月三日

二十歲生日 于美國教堂山窩所

Calligraphy by Wei Zhi-ji on his grandson Alvin W. Gao's painting – the "Peony" for the celebration of his own 20 years' birthday in Chapel Hill, NC in 1988 in USA.

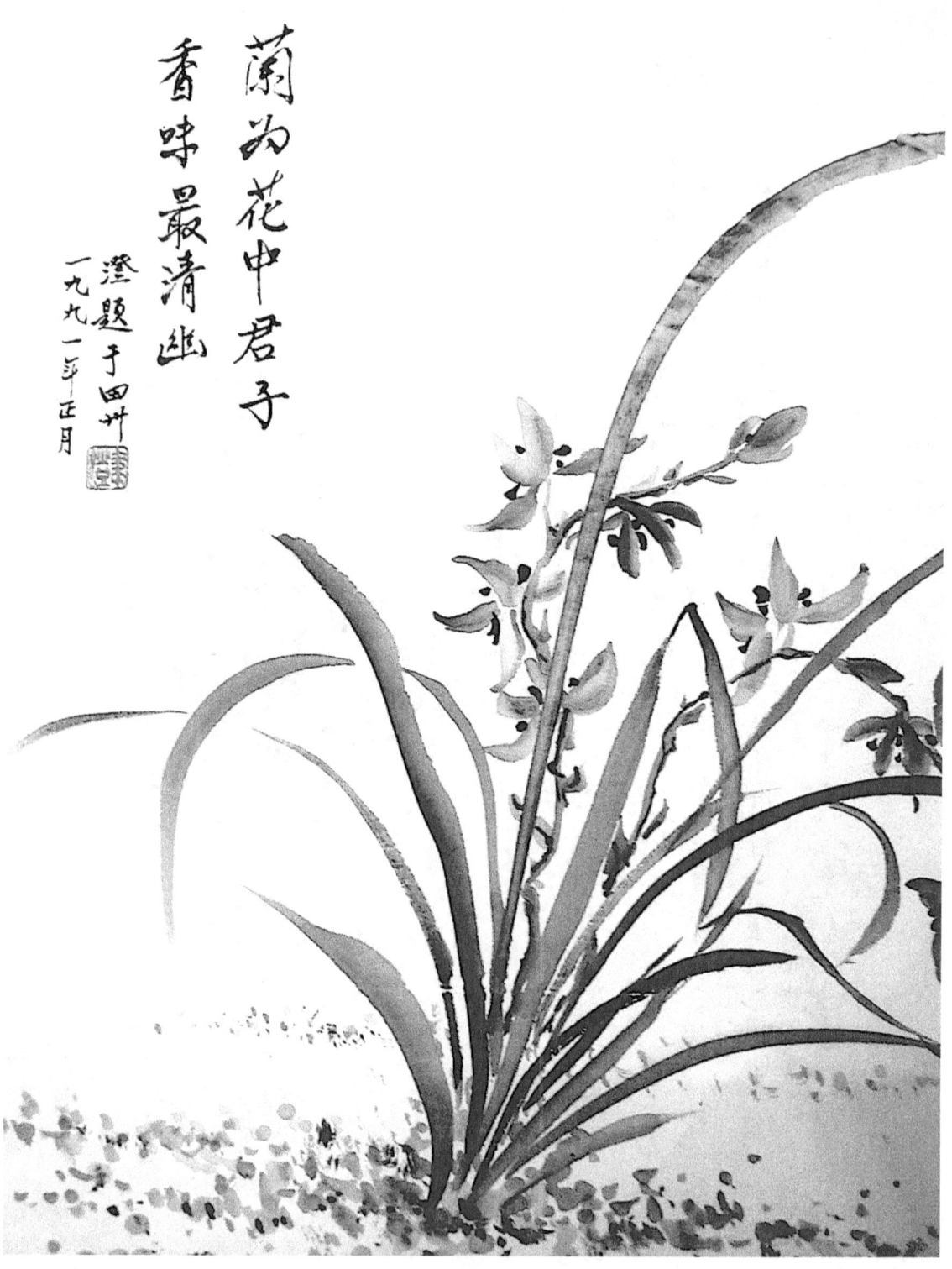

蘭為花中君子
香時最清逸
澄題于四川
一九九一年正月

3.2. Catherine W. Gao's calligraphy in the left part of Johnson K. Gao's color ink painting "Orchid and Grasshopper", written in Knoxville, Tennessee, USA, 1991.

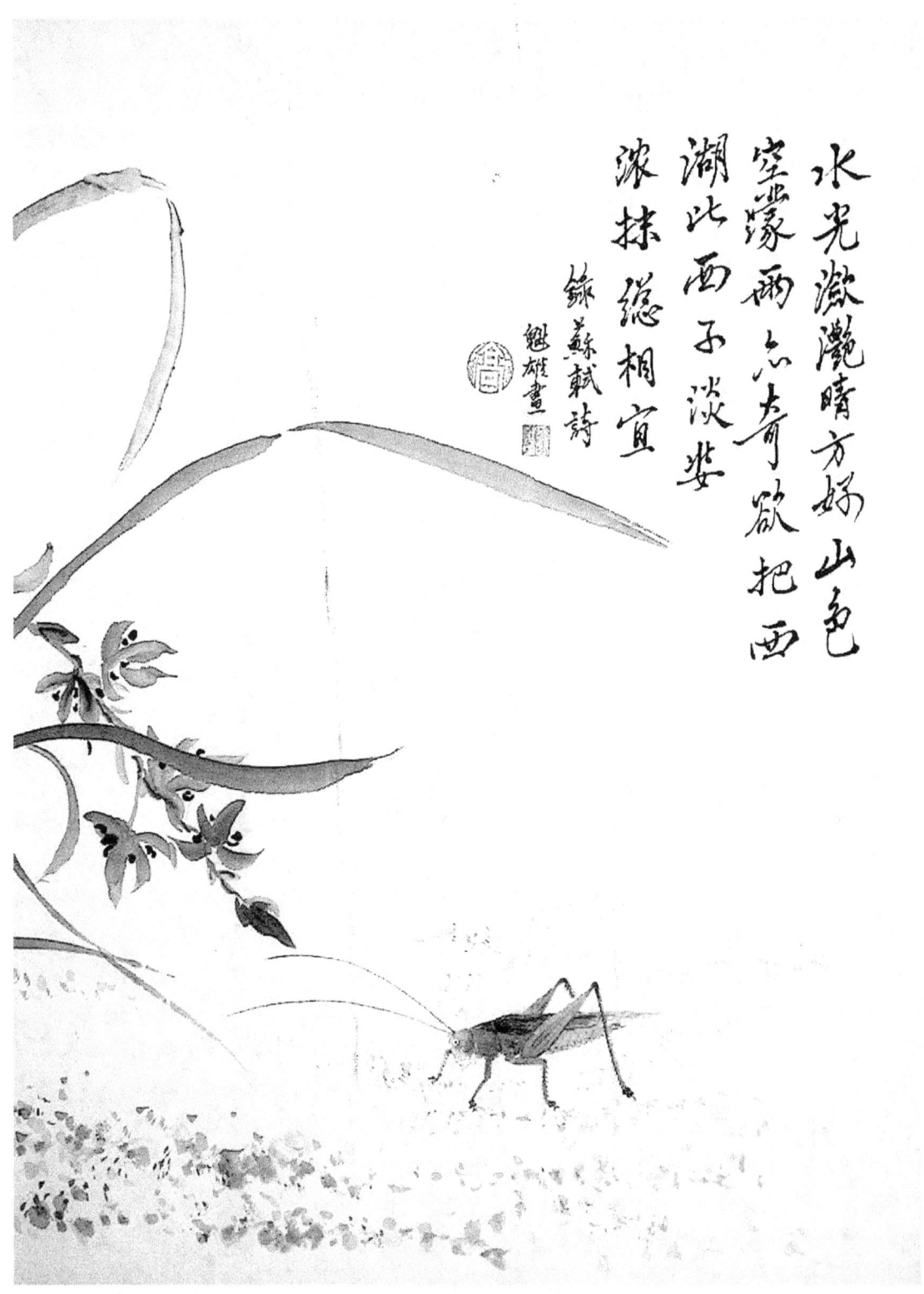

水光瀲灩晴方好　山色
空濛雨亦奇　欲把西
湖比西子淡妝
濃抹總相宜
　　錄蘇軾詩
　　繼雄畫

Calligraphy of Su Shi's poem by Johnson K. Gao in the right part of his own painting "Orchid and Grasshopper", painted in Knoxville, Tennessee, USA, 1991.

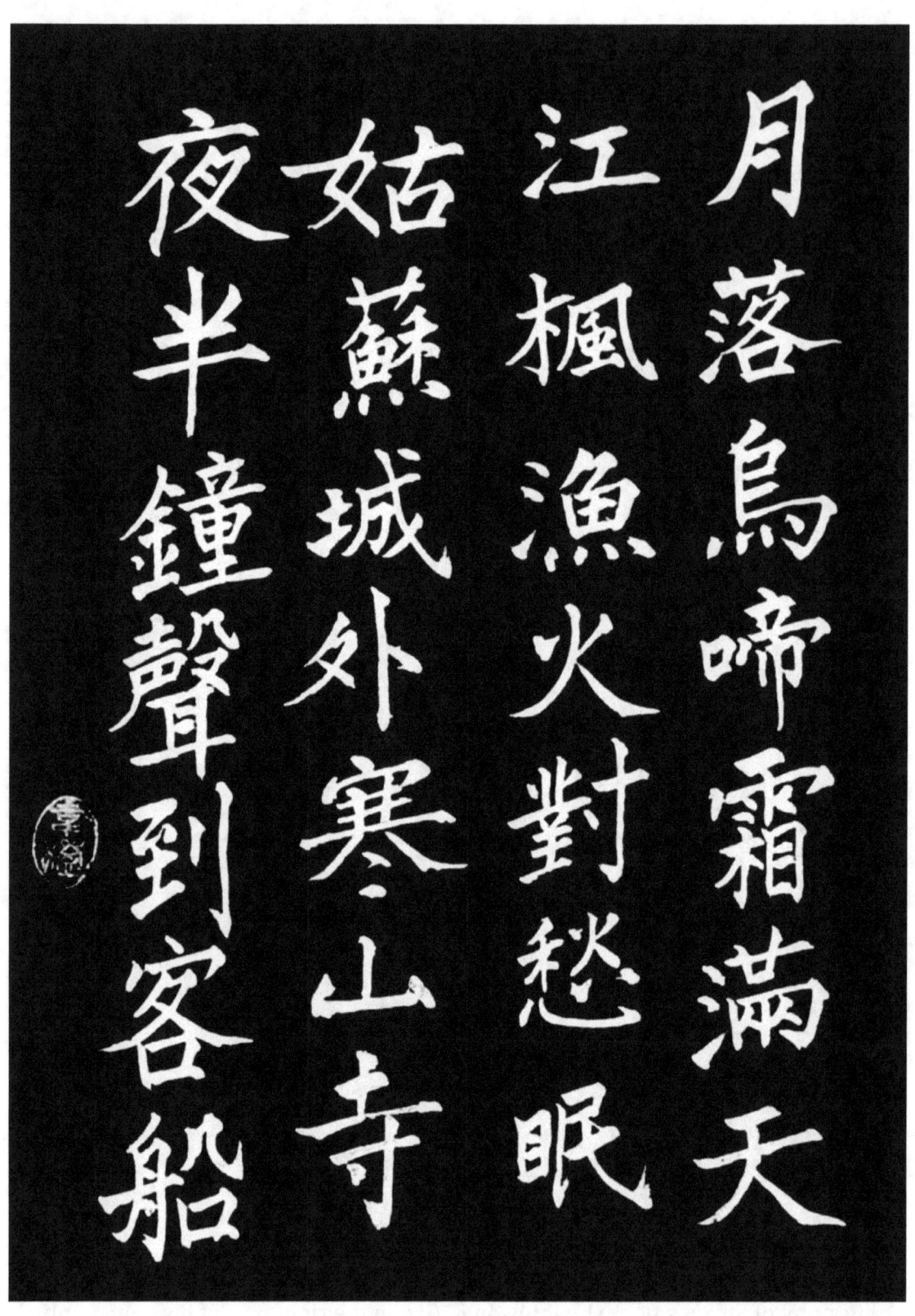

Calligraphy of Zhang Ji's Poem "Night Parking" by Catherine W. Gao (Wang Bang-shou's Grand-daughter, or, Wei Zhi-jie's daughter), written in Dallas, Texas, USA, 2011. (Inverted color)

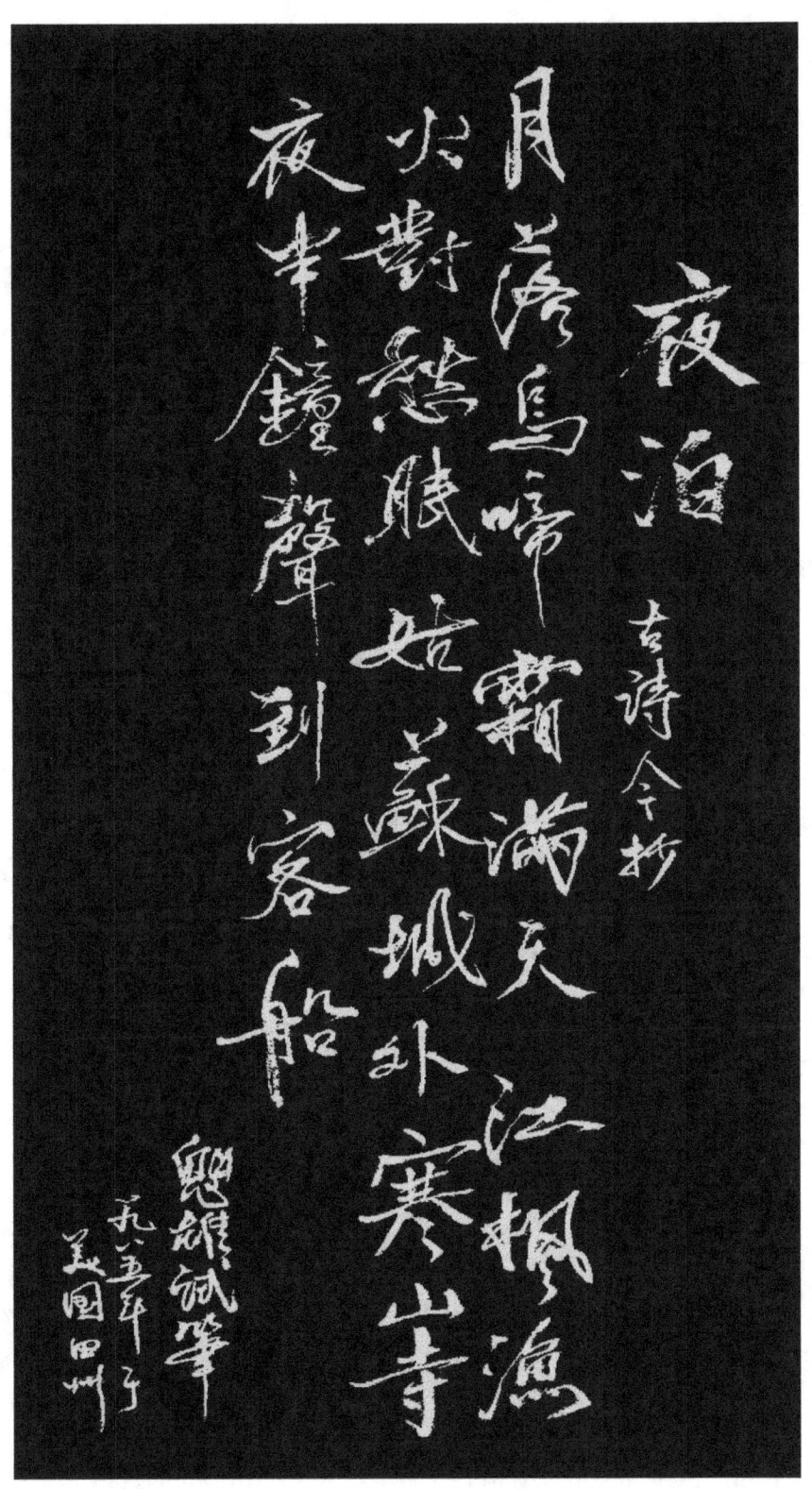

3.3. Calligraphy of Zhang Ji's Poem by Johnson K. Gao (Wang Bang-shou's grandson-in-law, or, Catherine W. Gao's husband), written in Knoxville, Tennessee, USA, 1985. (Inverted color)

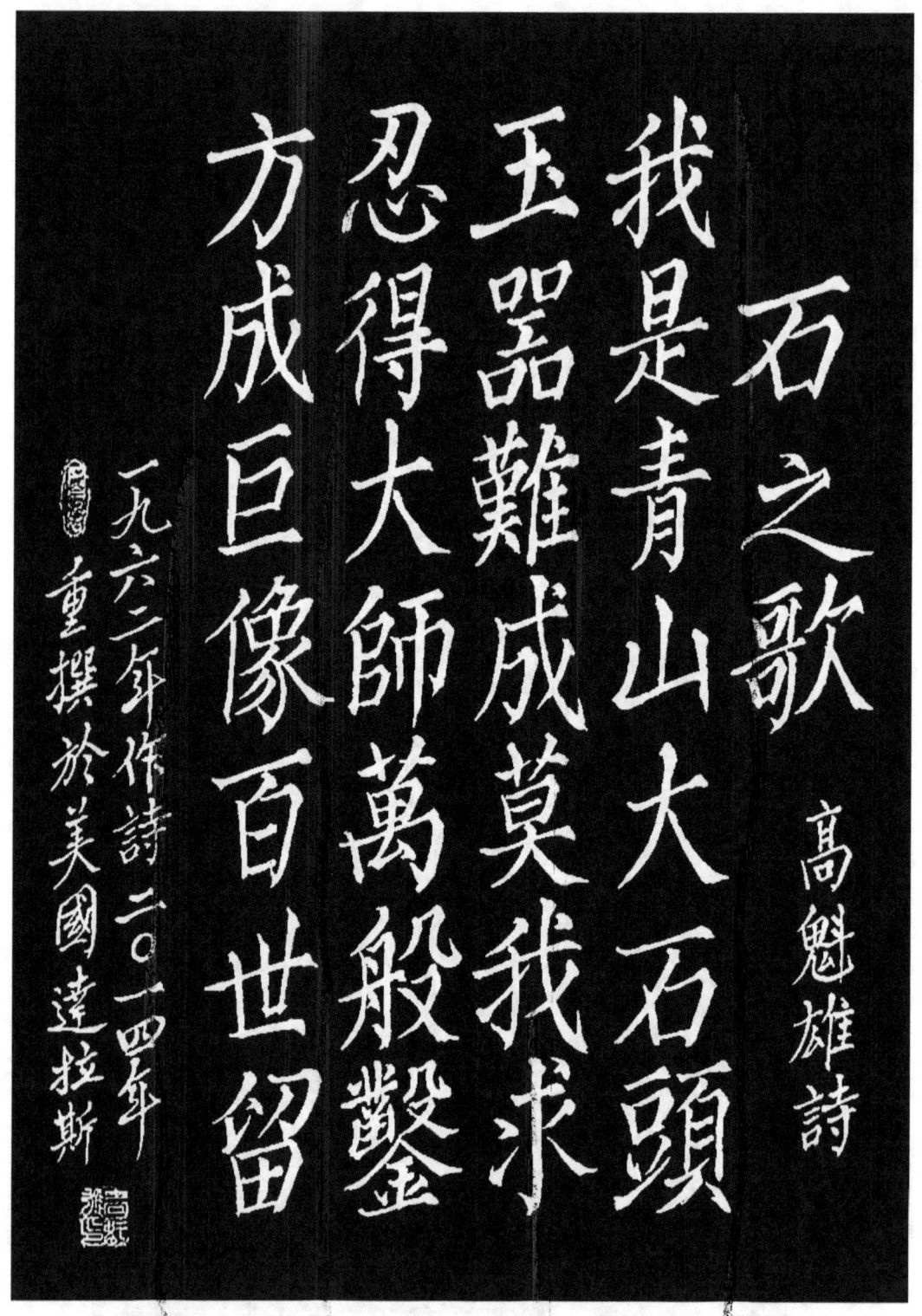

石之歌

我是青山大石頭
玉器難成莫我求
忍得大師萬般鑿
方成巨像百世留

高魁雄詩

一九六二年作詩 二〇一四年
重撰於美國達拉斯

Calligraphy by Johnson K. Gao in 2014 at age 77 in Dallas, Texas, USA, for his own poem "Stone Song", which was composed in 1962 in Shanghai, China, when he was 25 years of age pursuing a Ph D in Immunology and Developmental Biology in Chinese Academy of Sciences in Shanghai.
(Inverted color)

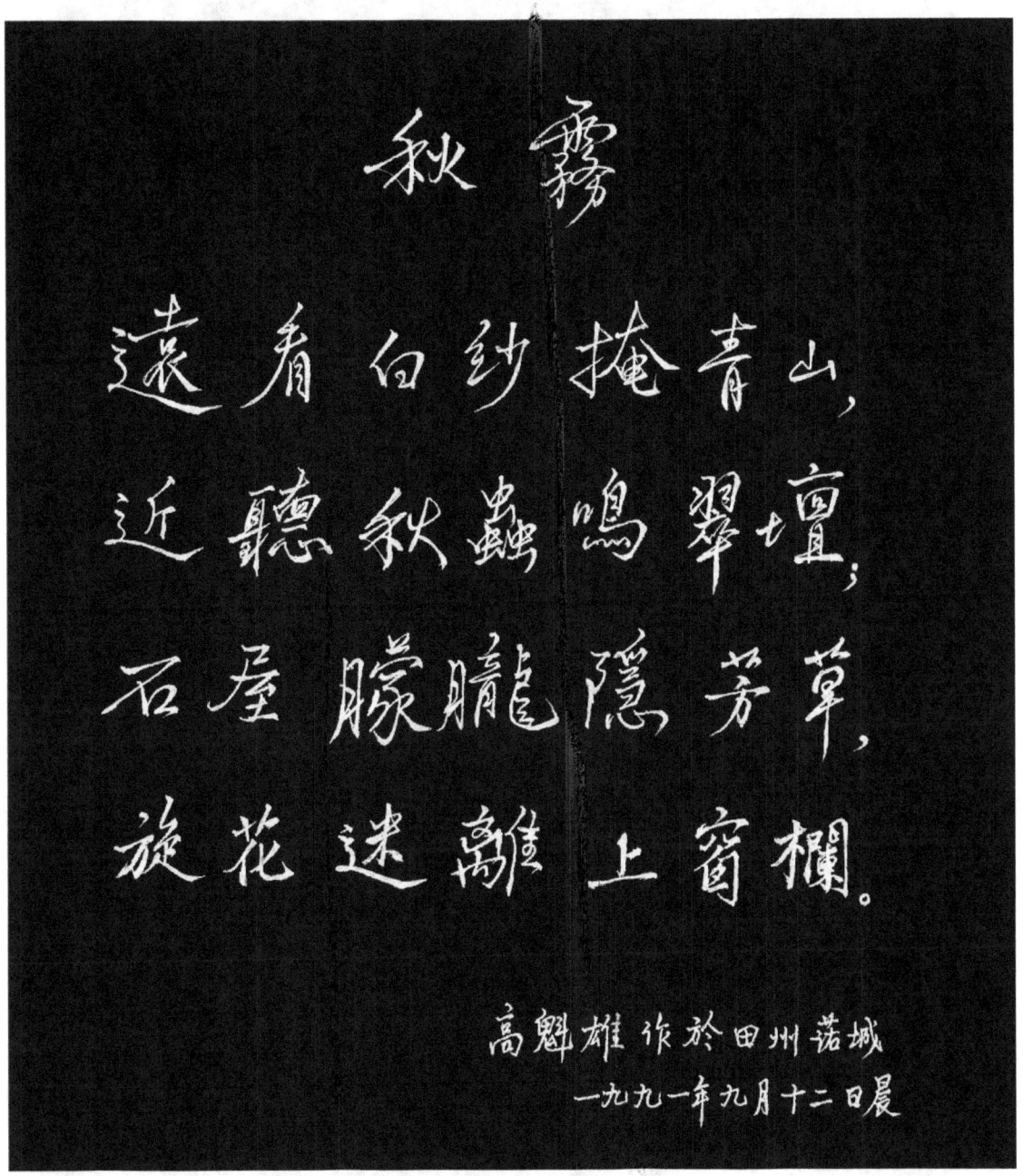

Johnson K Gao's poem - "The Autumn Fog" with 28 Chinese characters. It was composed on September 12, 1991 in Knoxville, TN, after a thick fog that day. Read it from left to right, upper to lower. (Inverted color)
It was translated in English by himself on October 18, 2014 as shown below.

Hills are blocked by the milky fog.
Crickets are singing under the green bed.
Fuzzy stony houses are hiding among woods.
Blurring flowers across the window are climbing up.

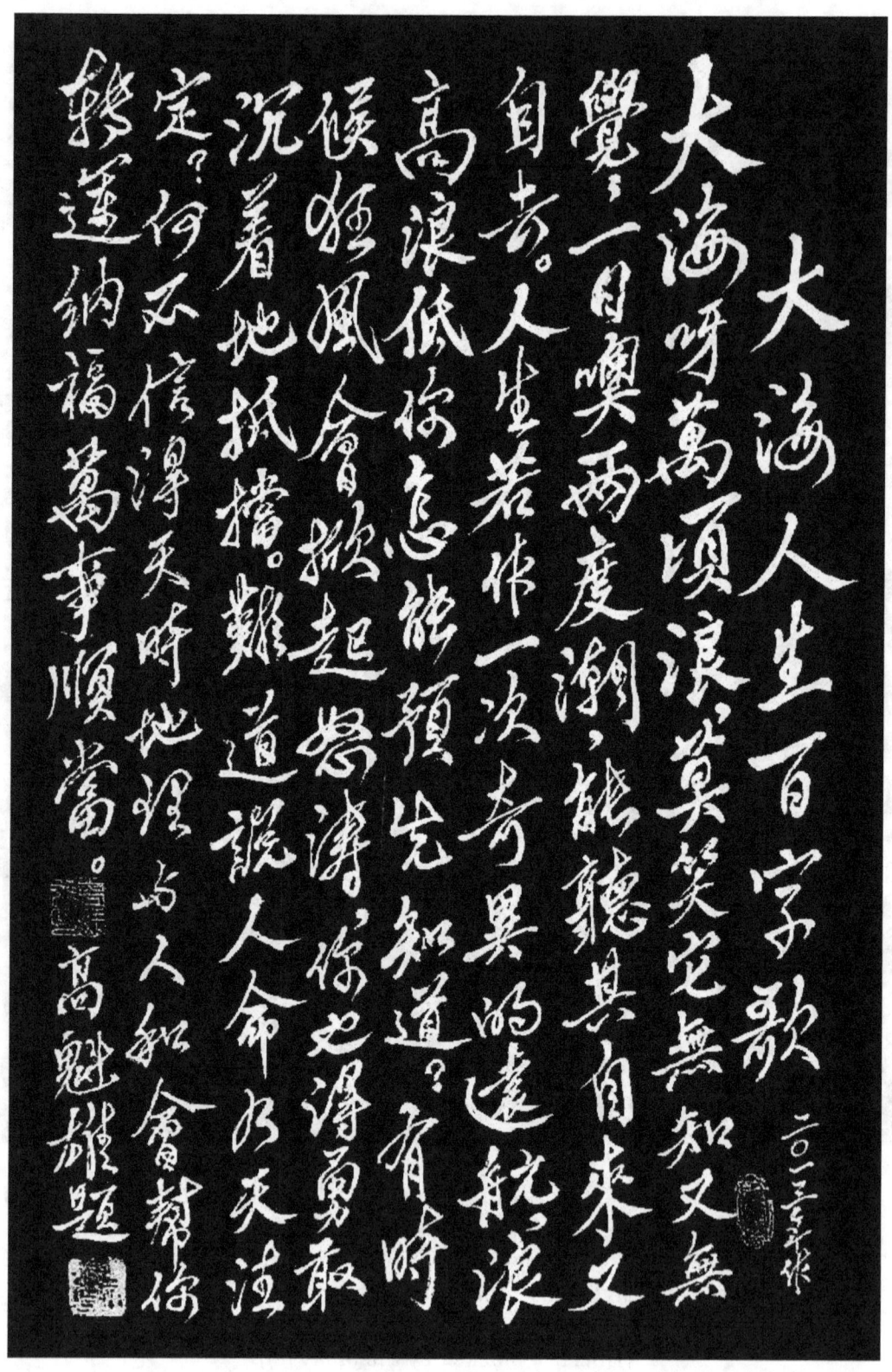

Johnson K. Gao's self-written poem - "One Hundred words on Sea and Life" finished in December 2013, Dallas, Texas, USA. (Inverted color)
(It needs to delete one word, such that number 32, to get the word count of 100.)

74

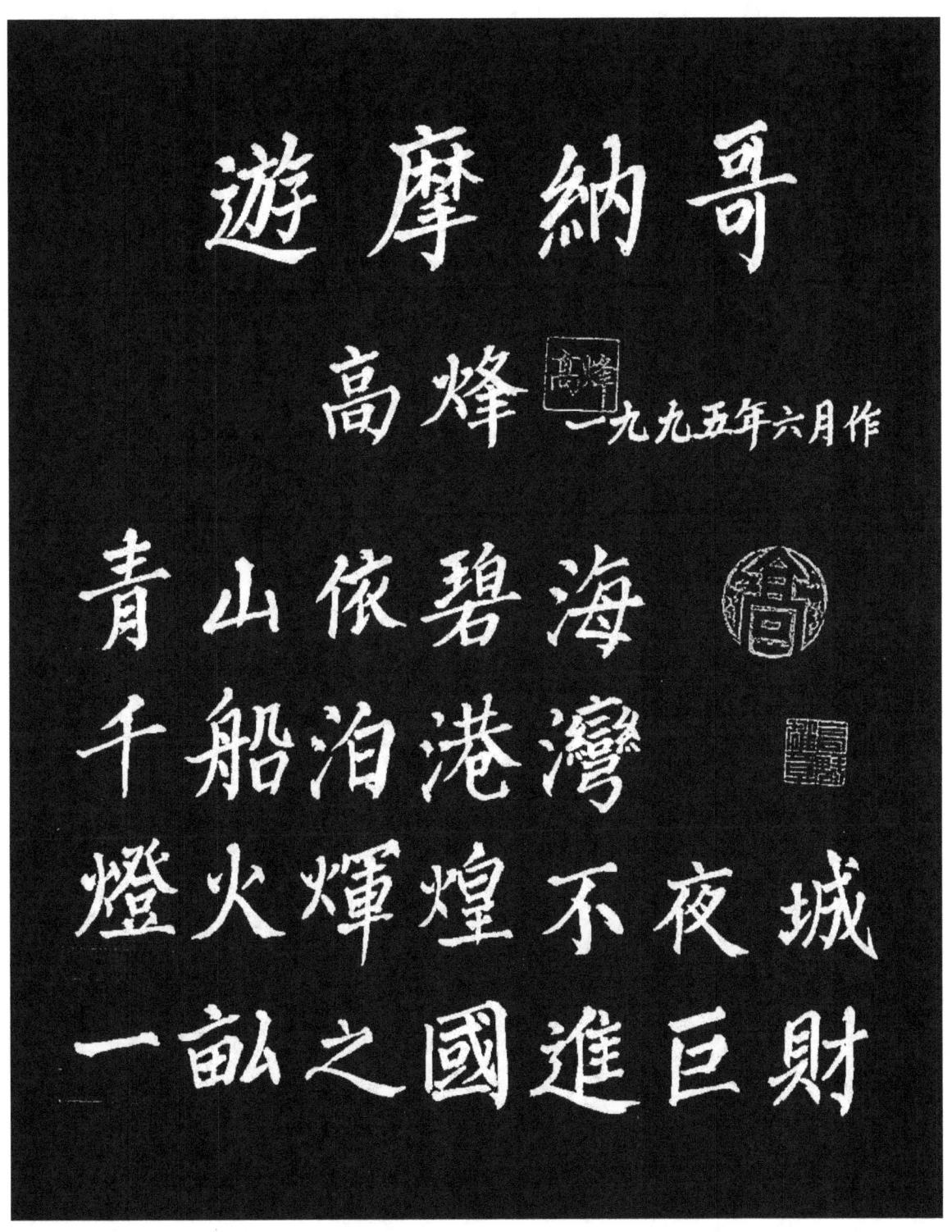

遊摩納哥

高烽 一九九五年六月作

青山依碧海
千船泊港灣
燈火輝煌不夜城
一畝之國進巨財

3.4. Calligraphy of Raymond F. Gao's self poem "Monaco" after he visited European eight countries in 1995. (Color inverted. Read it from left to right, upper to lower.)

www.ingramcontent.com/pod-product-compliance
Lightning Source LLC
Chambersburg PA
CBHW080819170526
45158CB00009B/2466